Innocent Postcards

Poetry * Ciphers * Verse

John Pietaro

Edited by George Wallace

Roadside Press

Acknowledgements

My greatest thanks to George Wallace for his editorial foresight, guidance and inspiration as well as the unsparing whip brandished throughout the creation of this volume.

And my deep appreciation also goes to Michele McDannold and ROADSIDE PRESS for believing in this collection. The literary underground lives on---well and thriving---within their catalog.

This book, and every creative effort I produce, is for Laurie Towers, my incredible life partner and wife who never allows me to quit in the face of adversity.

Innocent Postcards: Poetry, Ciphers, Verse is ultimately dedicated to the cultural workers whose creative visions and unceasing activism offered the people a fighting chance during each epoch of institutional repression. At the expense of democracy, the so-called invisible hand of capital has worked to divide and conquer within this American experiment; the mission of artists, brandishing truth, rebellion, and expression, has always been the tonic.

Introduction

The Cold War's decades of imperial espionage, manipulation, racism, antisemitism, homophobia, censorship, blacklisting and union-busting was only made bearable by the efforts of bold writers, musicians, actors, dancers, and visual, film and performance artists who risked careers and lives for justice. No easy task; after all, this nation was founded of, by and for the select few: ruling class, property-owning, white male slave-masters. The only Americans who had the vote. U.S. history is a sordid one.

But the structure that produced (convicted criminal) J. Parnell Thomas and his House Un-American Activities Committee, and (publicly shamed liar and defamer) Joseph McCarthy's Senate Sub-Committee was actually birthed with the industrial revolution, alongside capitalism's permanent fear and loathing of socialism. U.S. governmental oppression of the Socialist Party, founded 1900, the Industrial Workers of the World, founded 1905, and particularly the Communist Party, 1919, was tirelessly fought in the streets, courtrooms and media, and always in the company of cultural workers---the complete list of which would require multiple annotated volumes.

For the record, the Red Scares of 1919, the 1930s, and of course the McCarthyite derangement starting with 1947 and lasting through the Reagan '80s, is well documented. This collection seeks to recall the poison and commemorate visions, memories, emotions and the decided fight-back of the century. And more.

Within you'll swoon to Spanish Civil War ballads, struggle through the evening news, groove to progressive jazz, ponder black-and-white film and television, cringe at the headlines and advertisements and ride raucous punk and no wave. Also, marvel over seemingly mysterious reports on the global spy reality of the day, obtained through official channels: the FBI has so willingly offered its vault (well, the declassified one, anyway) for our reading pleasure. The reports on rock stars and the Rowan and Martin *Laugh-In* show would be purely comical were the level of ignorance not so repulsive.

Oh, and the title? The "innocent postcards" overtly sent via airmail included cryptic messaging that might otherwise appear, well, innocent. "Wish you were here" could imply much for agents in deep cover. You'll also find other tid-bits of the spy-vs-spy years tucked into these contents. Pay particular attention to the excerpts of reports between Bureau field offices and despotic leader, J. Edgar Hoover.

None of it should serve as comforting nostalgia.

-John Pietaro, Brooklyn NY

How About You?
(After the Bill Evans recording *Conversations with Myself*)

Hmmmmmm, light, seeking, hold, seeking

Don't mistake me for the laughter, the party's in the lounge.

Don't, don't. Mistake me,

Don't.

The buzzing hum, not with,

Not withstanding,

Not.

UP, over, up

Octaves stretching,

Further, beyond , I'm fine,

I'm fine, I'm..further…

How about, how about how, how   about   you?

Grappling over, barreling beneath, through courses of courses.

Courses of augmenteds, reaching

Flat 9s. Courses…//

Courses of curses…

Suspensions, leaping over leaping without leaping without leaping without reins

>*How….*

>>>*Don't mistake me, d-don't mistake--*

>*How about*

Don't

>>>*Spin, spinning, eyes releasing*

Spin severing

>>>*Careening insertion, degrading enflaming, dejecting, digesting, love infesting*

>>*MY CORE, ONCE IMMACULATE.*

Only one.

One with the sky just now.

Bourbon on Blue-Collar Ice

Scent of bourbon on ice, slice of orange, possibly,

Sits on tongue and nose as

Distortion paints the road

And arrows point on, afar,

      Fading airwaves and

      Echoes of Bowery at Bleecker.

      Smoking Hammond still calls to

      The least of voices, 48th and 8th.

Tones displaced,

post-Orwell demanding,

 Harmonies beyond meters,

   Pulse as unfelt on any wrist

    Wrested from old jukes

     Lost to decades of turbulence and rage

Pulse as unfelt on any wrist

Wrested from old jukes

     Lost to decades of turbulence and rage

When blood, too, flowed,

an uproarious babel;

Blurred beat, Mesmer phase.

We've never cried out who and why

but the skies bear witness:

there wasn't an America so knowing and

So of the populace

Regardless of what Jefferson wrote and signed, denied.

Here, reverb's echo plasters streets beneath.

What is left of Burroughs'
Bowery?

What became of
Alphabet City?

Fuck the power and

Eat the rich through

Days of Reagan and Bush and Trump's autopsy.

-June 30, 2023, 9:45pm, from a barstool at the Brooklyn Firefly

A Mountain Chain of Moments
(after Mayakovsky)

His verse by labor

Broke the mountain chain

This chain of a lifetime's howling

The rebel who spoke loudest

Whispered where professed,

Scattering links overground,

Writing at the pinnacle of primal hunger.

His verse by labor

Broke the mountain chain

This chain of long months lost, long days leaden

Oaths absent, promise befallen

The deceit of suffrage

The severing of tongue

Stilling of pen

Can never confine

Testament.

5

His verse by labor

Tore the mountain chain

This chain of moments begotten

And dreams deferred, he said.

And, look:

The skies above New York burn in

Pale scarlet.

-6/9/23, 12:02am

Of Mariupol

They witnessed the savior himself board that last train, the

Western force, this faceless deity,

Yellow, blue the profile, regrettably seen

Hands touching upward, out,

Reaching beyond northern waters where

Kalmin's River once released gold.

The Donetsk oblast,

Rank in its irony and

Festering in all frenzy

And the mortal city, back

To the coast, loss of retreat,

Sacrificed, to storm those below.

So many lives

torn by malice,

sliced by greed.

The bloodshed of '17

dank, still, on battlefields,

manifestos tossed.

Bastard sons of

Past revolutions

Forgotten.

Can you hear baying

From the abandoned lands?

-May 15, 2023, 8:43pm

Round Midnight
(After the Bill Evans recording, *Conversations with Myself*)

The night

   THE NNNNN

Night

   Spinning

The..

   Mmmmmmm, mm-mmm mmmm

                         Always night around here, though isn't it?

Night's air. "Night's Air"

   And each moment slows, slows

Burning inwardly and

And

And singstinging of Monk.

                         Always night 'round here, always.

                             I cannot find the light

The dancer is the dance, the source of

   The moon. See how it sizzles, spinning?

                             It sizzles

Doo-bop-da-da, da, dee-dah…

Showering sparks of sunlight and

And

THIS

    And

      THIS

                  And

Phantoms of lost dawns,

(Phantoms) (Phantoms) (Phantoms) (Phantoms)

                LOST dawns, he said..

spirits in, in, in

IN the never known, never begone

    shhhhhssss

Scent of night becomes

    Heart's darkness

You, Ruby.

You, Ruby ---

Scent of sense and *YOU, Ruby.*

> You, as all falls quiet. You through darkened eyes.

To inhale is to inspire, downtown turns, downtown turns,
so shhhhhssss

No, it's not yet late. Not yet.

> *The citysky is overwhelming from here, though.*

> - No, not just yet, not so late-

Simply 'round midnight, not the blue of the night

And the sky's thousand glances out.

> *The citysky is overwhelming from here, though.*

The thousand glances… pouring trances…

> *The city*

> Simply overwhelms, overwhe…..

> *--Shhhhhsssshhhout not so blue,*

Not so blue your darkened eyes

S o f t l y

S o   s o f t l y   n o w.

G o   s o f t l y   n o w.

Of Parnell, Richard, and Roy
(For the Hollywood 10, Rosaura Revueltas, Bertolt Brecht, and Rod Serling)

Can you still,

can you still see

see through to

the timelessness, our duration,

Timepiece notwithstanding,

Torrents,

static in orbiting streams, grey over greying.

Minute findings; and the screen visitation: the ghost, that
snow.

Play with the rabbit ears, why don't you?

*

**Are you now or have you ever been
a member of the
communist party?**

*

Jesus Christ, the memories are upended, yet the
station breaks for commercial messages remain.

12

This was always the point.

*

<u>Mr. Trumbo</u>: I believe I have the right to be confronted with any evidence which supports this question. I should like to see what you have.

Oh. Well, you would!

Yes.

Well, you will, pretty soon.

*

Can you, can you, can you still

Hey be careful,

you'll blow a fuse! And

*

(pounding gavel):
The witness is excused. Impossible.
<u>Mr. Trumbo</u>: This is just the beginning—

(pounding gavel):
Just a minute—
--of an American concentration camp

*

13

This never seems to get old. Not like us. Not like

black-and-white lives.

From 'Buy Russian War Bonds' to containment,

C.O.N.T.R.O.L.

Listen, there's the noontime air-raid.

Can't you quite hear?

*

<u>Mr. Miller</u>: I am here to tell you what I know.
    Tell us what you know. Who invited you there?
I couldn't tell you. I don't know.

*

Timepiece notwithstanding,

messaging then was calling someone from the window or

leaving microfilm in a pumpkin…

*

**--Can you tell us who was there when you walked
into the room? These were Communist Party
meetings;
were they not?**

These were writers, poets, as far as I could see,
and the life of a writer, despite what it sometimes

seems, is pretty tough. I wouldn't make it any
tougher for anybody.
I ask you not to ask me that question.

*

The window,

the window remains still,

open, and we can just see through to the past.

It's a perfect view of then and

Can you imagine the …

*

<u>Mr. Miller</u>: I am trying to elucidate my
position on the relation of art.

You are directed to answer the question.

I have given you my answer, sir.

*

Can you, can you still hear

hear the words,

so raw, Greek chorus, uproarious in the gallery,

voice as razor, stare sublime.

*

15

(audience laughter)

*

Black-and-white the lives, ghosted,

steeped in drifts set whirling,

dreamlike, the miles, the hours,

drip paintings in luminous grey

*

**Did you collaborate with Hanns Eisler
in song uh In Praise of Learning?**

<u>Mr. Brecht</u>: Yeah, uh collaborate, I wrote
that song, he only wrote the music.

You wrote, you wrote the song.

I wrote the song.

**Would you uh, would you recite to
the committee the words of that song?**

Yeah, I would. May I point out that that song is, is
a, is... comes from, an, an adaptation I made of
Gorky's novel, The Mother, and in, in this song a
Russian worker woman advises other poor
people.

Uh, it was produced in this country wasn't it

Yes, '35, New York

Did you write that Mr. Brecht?

No, uh I wrote a German poem, but that is--- very different…from this thing… (audience laughter)

*

It's a perfect view of then and

Can you understand the

Can you see the words, yet?

Time's almost up, she keeps calling and we keep on laughing………………..

*

Some people did ask you to join the Communist party, didn't they?

<u>Mr. Brecht</u> - uhh…

*

And we can just see through to the past.

This never seems to get old.

Not like us. Not like us.

Welcome the Saber

Belief taking leave in that moment of decision.

Choice, but not choice whether to

Remain or not remain. How do we,

How to keep——--

And they welcomed the next life,

Lifting chins high for the saber.

"Its blade has been cut very fine", she explained
sedately.

"Sharp like a razor.

So, there will be no pain at all."

As one then another throat was severed.

I watched the flesh separate,

Exposing the blush, steaming geysers running

Down one, then another's neck and chest.

Each participant appeared tranquil as they became
cleansed, emptied.

Thankful utterances were distorted only by

The generous deep red flow

spilling back in, coating the larynx.

> "Never before", she assured while crossing herself,
> "Could so many know serenity in one gathering."

> And the lines of the people grew only

> Longer, much longer,

> With thriving enticement.

You may have heard the very air that day felt softer, softer than ever before, softer even than anyone could remember.

Caressing breezes on the face verged on the erotic, with nerve-endings dancing in national pride and titillation.

The woman's detachment, raven hair pulled back tightly, her full gaze into the eyes of the dying coupled by a compassionate petting of the cheek, reflected the touch of the affable wind on that perfect day.

> *In the moments before surrendering*

> To the horizon, the sun splintered into

> Angular beams, turning gold all in reach.

> Greyness then came up from under, enmeshing with

> The copious puddles

> Of drawn blood

Now turned purple with

The coming evening's

Cool.

Darkness, that day,

Not only fell,

It was befallen.

Cold Wars and Some-Thousand Clowns

Murray Burns, acerbic, singularly bohemian writer who shouts early-morning insults to the wealth of The City.

Writer! A *Writer!* How magical the word, the boy thought,

How special the mission…

Publicly declaring his intended profession, the boy tread boldly, reading aloud for an audience of classmates, teacher and the school administration.

Assistant Principal Zeppelin, stuffed suit and toupee, up front in a third-grade desk all the more miniature about his sizeable girth,

Young, attractive Mrs. Schengel, perched upon her desk, silkened legs on full display and

The boy felt like Sinatra at the Sands.

"That's a fine job, a fine job", Mr. Z exclaimed in his bloated, smiling face, maneuvering awkwardly out of the seat.

"Let's have another big rrrround of applause (he always stressed the width of the word "rrrround") for our young author, here".

It was a moment.

SUDDENLY, AN INTRUSIVE, DEAFENING RING TORE THE ATMOSPHERE.

Mrs. Schengel, back in her dangling heels, directed everyone into the hallway. Maintaining size order, the children rushed into the hall, squatting in place, hands over heads: this the prescribed safeguard against atomic assault.

Oddly, the bell continued to resound and resound, piercing the suddenly icy air, a near physical striking. The children, shivering, wrapped arms around knees, hands over ears. Some were rocking in place in an errant self-soothing attempt, but the racket only rode the chilled wind. With smoky, visible breath, hair askew, Mrs. Schengel cried out to Mrs. Oland,

"Isn't that damned bell supposed to eventually stop?!".

But Mrs. Oland couldn't hear her for the

harangue now ringing in advanced harmony,

trumpeting augmented, clangorous, air-raid volume. And the children screamed as sheets of sound cast a painful, demanding swath.

And Mrs. Schengel, crouching in formation, eyes tightly shut, prayed aloud,

begging one entity or another to stop

the bomb from dropping onto Brooklyn.

***

BUT THE RINGING PERSISTED
and finally woke him from near-rest on the couch.

Awakening with a start, latest deadline due, he peered around the room, momentarily

Flustered. The wall clock read 2:32 AM.

It's later than he thought.

Window directly above open precariously wide, the cool autumn air had stiffened enough for the

Aging writer to recall the eight-year-old facing nuclear annihilation.

He shut it soundly, closing out the cold.

But the ringing has yet to cease.

(Wasn't that Herb Gardner something?)

When Reagan was Bad

There was a time, wasn't there,

When Reagan was bad?

Real bad?

Teflon Don before there was,

His fruitless charm and B-movie grace

Arm in arm with Helms and Thurmond.

We died, laughing. We died by the millions.

                    Lifestyles of the Rich & Famous,

                      Transglobal vanities, sans savings.

                          No loans and, hey,

                    There's powder on your nose.

       You've still got Milken on your lips too, don't you?

And what of Bonzo at Bitburg laying wreaths

On Mag the Knife?

Remember? Remember when?

When Reagan was bad? Real Bad?

In the throes of Fallwells and Wildmons,

Schlafly's pulpit an October Surprise

Contra-indicating the Jessicas and Tammy-Fayes

Who kneeled deep for penance.

Remember when we the people were bad,

so bad they had to stop us? They told us so.

Remember when Edwin Mouse roared

"Entartete Kunst!"

As Mothers of Prevention vamped

Moral equivalents of Founding Fathers and

D'Amato squatted, expressing all over "Piss Christ"?

You know you do.

And when Rohrbaching Frohnmayer reamed out "Witness"

While licking chocolate off of Finley?

That Commission peered deep into Sprinkle and

Close-danced over Mapplethorpe's grave,

Their footprints piercing normal hearts,

Blackening eyes and souls to

Shutter mouths in St. Pat's,

But December first never arrived.

Just ask the angels.

> Galleries burnt, then, like flags, the ashes of
> Charred Reds and Jump Blues
> Scattered through our veins.
> Illegal needle exchange,
> A diocese of shredded dogma strayed
> Like lives where social service gone expired,
> Passé as voice, hollow as will.
> Some remember.

Gipper, you laughed, naming dues-paying names and

Whispering into Cohns of Silence, you,

Warrior in from the cold,

Shriveled smile buffed with saddle-soap,

Dressed in diamonds on loan.

> *Illegal arms for trade! Illegal arms!*
> *Step right up! Step right up!*
> We're mourning, we're mourning,

We're mourning all over America.

Gipper, your diaper filled with

The spill of tomorrow preserved

The shit of today…

Democracy for sale to the highest bidder.

They dug you out and propped you up with

Hollywood lights and market dregs,

These thoughtless charades combed over the rot

To cast the command performance

Fit for Narcissus. It's been 40 years, 45.

Your reign is but the shrapnel. Go away; go the fuck away.

Remember when Reagan was, when Reagan was…

When life fluttered over the Stock Exchange balcony,

Loose cash inciting to riot and the

Butcher's bill called in the payment.

A nether day.

There was a time, that time,

One we remember.

But this day, today, we live

It again.

Now, Nicaragua is Mexico and

Dying queens, the new immigrants.

Conspiracies are heritage as

Charlottesville chants

"So Proud of Your Boy",

Mask-less but hooded

For blood and soil.

Day undone.

We remember;

we can't help but.

Yet, still

We die.

We die,

We die laughing.

What Did They Do to Billie?

What did they do to Billie?

Tell me: what did they do?

G-Man ate her flesh and

Straight jacket held her, frenzied.

They disappeared her voice,

Dropped it on an off-ramp,

The one took Bessie.

And what did they do
to Bird---

Turned tacit inside.

They stole the muse
from Monk,

Beat Miles blind at Birdland's door.

Shuttered Langston at the crossroads
of

HUAC and Red Channels Avenue.

Tell me, what did they do?

Ornette, bum rushed out of L.A. and

Ayler dispelled to the East River.

Lee Morgan lies bleeding at Slug's;

Always waiting

for the snowed-in ambulance to arrive.

Here's to the magical, lived incomplete.

Here's to the justice, never delivered,

Here's to the sediment of the new

that lies lingering

Still

on the tongues of poets.

Tell me: how did they do it?

Down to 30 Seconds of a Beat
(for Umbra and Tompkins Square)

Jaws grinding down on the swing,

  Eyes tight, slight flutter,

    Shut out the grey dimming light;

      Head well down in thunder as hands grapple for

The spaces unseen.

Breathless, breathless, breathe.

Harmonic clouds, cluster of burning tinder,

Scent of the faintest outline rendered…

It's not yet blue, the backdrop.

Flaming scarlet hue above.

Each flicker of black and red

leans deep into the unfolding.

Hands tandem, then, tandem.

So widely spaced,

The hollow season,

Singing its hard solemn song,

31

Ancient, away, the mystic
Purple artesian well, flowing

Tears unseen; Spring, spring is,

Spring is here,

Must be here;

Spring must.

Spoils of SoHo

Nist,

Niente, this emptying of all

expectation, this scraping blank

of the artist's canvas, that

poet of the drumsticks splintering,

this plastic saxophone

of the unreconstructed underground,

Nist,

Niente, these no-wave teeth,

biting deep into the vinyl grooves, that

metal to metal, soiled harmony

lipstick to lip, this

downtown burning.

scent of leather,

flooding of pores

 Nist,

Niente, artist writhing in

the unspilled underground,

standing empty before

the vestal creation,

scrape blank the canvas,

disturb the comforts and

paint free the jazz vexation.

Blake Dreams of Duke
(After the Ran Blake recording *Duke Dreams*)

Shhhhh, that's Ran Blake dreaming of Duke.
Academic radical's calling

Campus fire as Edward Kennedy Ellington's voice
surrounds

 the pianist's lips, emoting from within.

Maintaining hands, minor seconds' ornamentation, the
bluest tri-tones and,

Get this: that darkness which follows Blake even in silence

Is now dressed in a gold-trimmed white tuxedo.

Fit for the Cotton Club.

Black and Tan, the Fantasy, scooping up field hollers left
behind,

Spilled over lifetimes

brief, urgent and god damned, this

 modernism with just the subtlest

Swing.

Dazzle me with royalty, a near two-step

quivering stance,

Duke as legend, hot August, those nights.

Restricted.

Supper served

before the first set

…in the kitchen of course, as

Autograph hounds greet him at

the colored-only entrance.

Langston wrote of wealthy whites

at "ringside tables staring at the Negros".

Forget the A train; have the chauffeur drop me off

Uptown.

Harlem: all the rage for Park Avenue money,

Privileged curiosity.

What Depression? We're partying to jungle music, so

Grease up those spot-lit torsos and

Order me a Death in the Afternoon. Make it strong.

Aerial the dancers over Sonny Greer's pulse. Johnny
Hodges' alto mixes

It up with Juan Tizzol's trombone and, muted,

Bubber Miley's most sonorous trumpet lead.

Riches, riches flowed

Flowed in sound, always

     through Duke's sax section…

             Ran hears and reports it all

        with dancing hands, overworked stretches
           well beyond the octave.

           A quiet restlessness,

Covert pangs and near-hidden rage in Sophisticated

       Lady leaps of an 11th toying with

         upper register's half-steps,

          black over white,

     chord crushes, delicate, echoing lonesome.

Blake dreams

Dreams of Duke, late the ventures

Calls the watchman;

sounds through a transom, soft moans in the dark,

noise from an airshaft and

smoke rising.

Black as if bereav'd of light.

And there are tygers burning bright.

Discreet Foundlings of Quiet Places (for Lou Reed)

Velvet dragged

Splintered by words

Shredded intention,

Split by narration,

Dull blade of secrets

                  Vexed, haunted eyes,

                    The shaded view, lost,

                      the mirror, too,

                          and the downward gaze into

                            steaming black leather.

                        The droning, slow dragging,

                          step-time in dreams.

            Relentless rhythm, carry me;

                      steal this oxygen. Ignite.

                    Discreet foundlings of quiet places

Stories told, poached, sired.

                  But shhhh, never look to the faces.

Never see.

> Lit by shadow, Genet, Schwartz, Riley,

pathways bending far from sight. Sides

> split by feedback waltz darkly, as

bums of dharma sing praise and spite.

Wild tonearms' ride on

> brittle, parched lacquer,

> Music much later, later
than the night.

Love Theme from 'Spartacus'
(After the recording by Bill Evans, *Conversations with Myself*)

Sun's up.

Sun's over…slowly

Softly and

    Tender. So tenderly

Sun's up…

       I am, I am, I am

The emptiness in my breast is now

    Now

The melting, the placid, the warm bath lingers,

       Embrace what is golden

    Never to think. Never to see. Never to see over.

       I am, I am, I am…

The warmth of air touches me, ingrained

    Ingrained in my soul,

       My soul.

Not alone.   Not alone.

       I am.   I .

The Visitant

Faceless,
     Gripping hands in virtual expanse,
       Reigning rhythm and time.
            Skin metallic, rich
              expression of silver,
         hammered accent:
           deep red, blood orange

              Beaten purple.
                a
              groping.
          a bestowing.

            The Visitant.
       counterpoint of one
    Through the empty house,
  Sleepless, mute and stiffened.
   Tri-tones,
     gliding and violent
        percussives, turning electric,
           this storm of sound.

       Electric the novel,
           Electric the words
     postcards of verse and satori:
          flight of the fearless.

Savage skies.
a probing,
         a bestowing.
               Sleepless,

                    The Visitant
                         points north.
                              Or above.
                    "Or maybe,"

Claimed our man in Tangier, eyeing Paris,

     "Man is mutating,

          mutating fast", he said.

          "Mutating

               Fast."

("The Visitant" is a poetic interpretation of a Mark Kostabi painting, with additional inspiration from William Burroughs and Adrian Belew; premiered in performance with Gene Pritsker's Composers Concordance at Kostabi World, NYC, 2023)

Our Words Are Razors

No nos moveran,

We shall not,

We shall not be moved.

We shall not.

Bottle-slide hovers battered frets,

Roadside off heritage trail.

And at last we end

the age of cant.

Wage slaves battle

World capital klan,

How much our flesh they feed upon.

Calloused hand over splintered neck,

It's a union drive

in a bourgeois town.

American worker defense,

weaponized,

long last, long last loss.

>   *Debout, les damnés de la terre*
>
>   *Debout, les forçats de la faim*

The voice a rasp, the cry of labor,

Fists aloft,

our words are razors.

At the Cellar Dog

Infernal space, torrid, dark.

Lurid its radiance in swelter and pace.

Cradling the chaser.

Howling with blue and white smoke

And quivering embrace.

Welcome the chasm, this

Piano-less four-tet:

Bell tone in tango with

Low crying reed. Such

Cleaving at the center suggests

Snow-filled nights. But

Winter still calls to the after-hours.

It's Mulligan and Chet, late-50s cool,

Rivaled by binges and pools of wine.

Two of the morning a Friday's revel,

Dipping and splashing yet gaming the noise.

A phantom of summer, this splurge of swing,

Infection, inflection, no matter,

Here in Christopher's wild depths –

So callow the singing -- these

Horns of the living.

Fade To White - *Long days, long past*

  I.   Look: Multi-colored

were the clouds of early

winter, rainfall dampening

heads, shoulders and

grounds; the rain thickened,

all across the campus

clocks chimed.

II. Listen: a furtive sound,

a roiling, chafing, awakening,

my pulse locked in on its

tempo, and I held on; sky

turned cobalt blue, blue

as some fallen star.

  III. *Scent* of carnation, return
                    to the burning sun.
                         Fade to white.

Louder, Please, My Watch Can't Hear You

In from the out, in

From the bitter, the boreal.

In from,

In from the Cold,

The Cold:

The crossing of nowise and misbegotten…

Betcha can't eat just one!

FEDERAL BUREAU OF INVESTIGATION. Reporting Office: New York, 4/8/60:

On April 6, 1960, "The New York Times" carried a full-page advertisement entitled "What is Really Happening in Cuba" sponsored by the Fair Play for Cuba Committee, offering to send "the truth about revolutionary Cuba" to anyone who wrote asking for information. In addition to chairman Waldo Frank, sponsors of the notice include Truman Capote, Simone de Beauvoir, Norman Mailer, Kenneth Tynan, John Paul Sartre, and James Baldwin

…Uniformly bygone.

Closed for business and

Beyond sight.

The exploding cigar: it simply can't miss.

We bring good things to life

The Glove Pistol for him

And for her,

The Lipstick Gun.

All I want all I want for all I want

For Christmas is the Dragonfly Insectothopter.

Look how good you look now

June 29, 1962

Subject: Norman Kingsley Mailer

-Security Matter – C

Mailer, 39, resides New York City and is in Section A of the Reserve index… characterized as an "offbeat crusader for peace"…admitted to being "a leftist". Charged the FBI with being a secret police and that it should be abolished. On television show 8-8-61 said that no one is happier than the FBI to see communism succeed in Cuba since it gives the FBI something to do.

In from out,

From the distant,

The bizarre,

Out from under,

From U.N.C.L.E.

May 1964

To: Director, FBI

From SAC, Tampa

"Laboratory is requested to determine if enclosed record, "Louie Louie" can be considered obscene for purposes of prosecution under ITOM statute"

In from the Cold:

The crossing of nowise and misbegotten,

Bygone by design.

Share moments.....Share life

3/26/67 The Monkeys (corrected: Monkees)

"This series features four young men who dress as "beatnik types" and is geared primarily to the teenage market. During recent weeks, the stars making public appearance tours…which, in the opinion of ██████ constituted "left-wing innovations of a political nature."

Bygone by ratings, or raidings,

It was always the beatnik reciting revolution.

So why can't we find the Kerouac or Burroughs files?

Absolutely no no no restitution.

And away go troubles… Down the drain

Los Angeles Field Office

NOTE: The record forwarded from ██████████ is by the Fugs. This group described as New York's most fantastic protest rock and roll peace – sex – grass – psychedelic singing group who write their own material utilizing the artistic and literary heritage of the low East Side of New York combined with the civil rights and peace movements…the record forwarded contains

11 songs which are vulgar and repulsive and are most suggestive.

March 26, 1969

Thank you for your letter of March 20th.

I, too, share your concern with this type of recording...

it is repulsive to right-thinking people and

can have serious effects on our young people.

Sincerely Yours,

J. Edgar Hoover

Deep down you want Hoover

Remember the 1919 Palmer Raids of the new

Bureau of Investigation, headed by young queen Hoover?

6/3/69 James Marshall "Jimi" Hendrix

"...well-known Negro entertainer. During May 1969, was arrested by the ████ after a quantity of marijuana was found in his shaving kit. He was charged with illegal possession of narcotics and at the present time is on $10,000.00 bail.

They cast the COINTELPRO to come,

The black bag jobs, blacklistings, Black repression,

Red squads, loyalty oaths, wiretaps, the

Flaying of careers, families and dissent.

You're soaking in it!

New York, NY, September 5, 1969

The Grateful Dead (it would appear that this is a rock group of some sort)...

Probable cause for Title III investigation: LSD originated through San Francisco, California from Grateful Dead...well known to DEA San Francisco.

 when ▮▮▮▮ initially filed.

Celebrate the moments of your life

March 8,1971 Re: "Rowan and Martin's Laugh-In"

Captioned individual telephonically contacted the Bureau on 3/8/71 and reported that he had been watching the Rowan and Martin Show on channel 4. According to ▮▮▮▮ the show was "making fun" of the FBI and Director.

...During captioned show, a particularly vicious attack was made by means of a "knock-knock" joke in which the answer to "who is there?" is answered by "Hoover". In reply to the question "Hoover who?" a play on words is made in the statement "Hoover heard of a 76-year-old policeman?" Another sick-type joke pertaining to the Director was an announcement that "J. Edgar Hoover retired one half-hour ago but will be back at his desk first thing in the morning."

Try and get a copy of Laugh-In from Mar. 8

H.

My wife.....I think I'll keep her

March 16, 1972 John Winston Lennon/Yoko Ono

INS has current address of St. Regis Hotel 150 Bank Street, New York City for both Lennon and his wife.

During Lennon and wife's current stay in the United States, they made public appearances, along with Jerry Rubin, on the Mike Douglas television show, February 22, 1972...Lennon appears to be radically oriented, however he does not give the impression he is a true revolutionist since he is constantly under the influence of narcotics…

Things go better with Coke

Communists, socialists, anarchists,

gays and lesbians, outspoken artists all

Persecuted by Hitler in '33, targeted as well by

Hoover and Dies and Hoover and Thomas

Hoover and McCarthy, and Hoover and Goldwater

And Hoover and Nixon and Kissinger and Daly and
Reagan.

Call in the Loyalty Review Board;

god save us.

I'd rather fight than switch

Blue Monk

(After the Bill Evans recording *Conversations with Myself*)

It's--all-Blue, in,

       The grey-

          Bluest of blue

             a-Bluest of blue

Terms, cobalt, in,

B-bllllbbb—sharpness of stones

             a-B-Bluest of blue

             a- B-Bluest of blue

    Fly, derive,

        B-bllll---

          a-Bbluest of blue

           Bblue

Eyes bright shut and my

 Self-im-age in

Close-up view.

          Touch

Me,

Bluest of you,

You

Flesh is alive, unseeing, feel

Can I sense a-look,

a-live?

Threeee

Hold

Me,

Daaark!

Youest of true,

Your flesh is to thrive, oh,

What-a-life-this-be,

Unfurl   me   the   rest

Disconnect, disconject.

How begin when

It's all but a lie?

How in hell when

It's all gone awry?

Blue-est of bl…

of blues

Bluest

Bluuuuue..aaand,

dejected in blue,

Only, lonely indigo.

On Repelling Ghosts

Off the surrounding waters / The liquid air blows cold

Its path of reckless wind / Purges the night /Breaking black.

I at river's edge see / Driftwood undertow /

Incisors of salt / Frosting autumns / Freeze the dawn.

Darkened ceaseless horizon's / Thickening sky ebbing soul /

Sirens asunder as / Mem'ry's storm burns /

Tempest begone / Tempest Be Done.

---Reed Goldtran, Hart Island, 1923

Turning dark, that autumnal breeze,

Seasonally chilled.

In turtleneck and worn denim, he

Walked long blocks from lonesome parking,

Accompanied by East River's raw calling. Yes,

Brooklyn gets it like that around the edges.

    The heels of ankle boots tapped at evening's yawn;

    But for the persistence of the wind, all was still.

    Just after 8PM, it was, and

The sidewalks already emptying. Streetlamps threw

Beams into darkness, crafting shadows along night walls.

His one prize was the book. The book. That book, the impossible find

Tucked deep into his shoulder bag.

Slightly diverting, he walked to the diner. It was always open.

The house stereo: early Miles. Mmmmmmmuted trumpet, open air

Careened along the ceiling like a magic carpet.

"I'm buying the drinks tonight", he said, looking around; but he was alone in the diner, other than the tired waitress whose nametag read 'Laura'. "Okay, yours are on me", he tried.   "I feel like celebrating."

With Laura's fleeting smile to guide him, the man continued, "I'm finally done with rewrites on my play, plus I ghost-wrote a well-paying essay---before deadline".

The man smiled, almost shyly. "ummmm, I'm a writer."

> The waitress numbly looked back, chewing gum, nodding: "Oh! Cool. But, hey what can I get you toni…"

"AND I just came across a very old, rare book.", he added, near shouting with pleasure. "You must know, that place on fourth avenue. The used bookshop. Would you like…to see it?", he asked, without ever looking back, carefully removing the book from his shoulder bag.

> "Yeah, but did you want to hear about our specials?", she asked. Laura's feet hurt.

"Self-published in 1923, it was, by a poet imprisoned on Hart Island. HART ISLAND, working the burial detail!"

> Laura looked back, perplexed, fiddling with her pad and pen. It had been a long shift.

"You know, Potter's Field", he exclaimed. "Imagine that. A hundred years ago, this was, lost to time, it was. And what a grim place to write poetry. This renews my hope for, uh…the transformative power of word!", he explained, beaming more than intended.

Tired Laura looked deeply into her order pad, hoping this information wouldn't serve as a tip.

A double, he'd asked for, of the good stuff. And it stood now at attention, having poured like caramel-brown gold. "To beautiful poetry", he said, raising his glass to Laura. "And to the poetry of time!"

> Laura crinkled her eyes back at the man and

> The good stuff kept flowing.

By the time supper was served, he was four rounds in. The man had, cautiously, already removed the book from his shoulder bag, longingly gazing at the simple cover.

REED GOLDTRAN. Even the name sounded like an anagram. Or an amalgam.

Reed Goldtran. Poetry. So spare, so simple, so emergent. Like an oasis.

"You know, Laura", he called out to the waitress, busily on the phone with a take-out order. "I could find no history on this guy Goldtran".

He breathed in the scent of a turkey club now laid out on his plate. "I'll bet this was one of a handful of copies printed. Finding it now was something magical. Magical."

What's lost to the passage of more than a century.

He looked to the counter, noting Laura knee-deep into the screening of "The Man Who Came to Dinner" on the house television.

Head spinning some, the man felt the need to continue: "You know, I studied at NYU and have been a poet most of my life", he recounted. "Three books published by sizeable houses, plus all those anthologies, journals, readings, but what in hell have I really done? Busting my butt trying to get dramas staged and working every awful job imaginable to get by. But here's this guy, this Goldtran,

Whoever he was, coming from nowhere, then disappearing back into it, and he somehow wrote *this* collection while incarcerated. A prisoner. Handling the internment of corpses. Haunting, huh?"

There was no response from Laura who'd finally slipped off her shoes to catch a moment's peace. As her tired legs went up onto the stool, she sought to rub out the headache growing all night.

The man stared hard into the book's first page, fading into the violins and oboe playing softly. "No", he said to no one. "This is poetry for repelling ghosts".

Supper nearly done, he sat back to drink in the solitary, but not silent, moment.

Shhhhhhh, wait: it's Charlie Parker and Strings, the music swelling in spiritual tapestry. Bird's saxophone sang out David Raksin's theme, his theme from "Laura" as the richness of sound took the room, the sky beyond rippled hazily.

Conjuring Laura.   Laura and the shadows.

Long lost writer Reed Goldtran is, in reality, a Pietaro doppelganger haunting the margins of his novel-in-progress *Of Seconds and Shadows*

Of Heroes and Monsters

En route to the war to end all, capitalism replaced
democracy, unleashing a fully armed market over its
children.
Now that was something.
Moms love it!
Dads love it!
Even the kids love it!
It's time to get yours now!

super beings,
master spies,
space adventures,
classic monsters,
enemy agents,
hot rods,
soap opera vampires decorated our
comic books, cartoons, toys, model kits, monster
magazines, bubble gum cards, glow-in-the-dark posters,
Halloween costumes, bedroom slippers, breakfast cereals,
lunchboxes, TV dinners, and cupcakes fortified by rousing
TV campaigns. Truth and justice.

They shined in day's light and hunted under
full murderous moons as The Cold War raged on, pumping
fantasy through parlors far and wide.

Sounds like science-fiction,
but guess again…

The experts said it was the American Century and
The American Century was good.
(At least for the well-heeled and the military industrial
complex)
The planet—and its heavens--were for the taking.

Forget Clay vs Liston, Mustang vs Camaro, Munsters vs
Addams, Yankees vs Pirates, Bates vs Little Rock, and
especially Loving vs Virginia, our new flag-waver was
G.I. Joe vs G.I. Kong.

In this corner: Uncle Sam, bloated with
war spoils and corporate reach, hell-bent
on saving the earth for profit; on that side
stood the Russian Bear with a million
eyes, pounding his shoe like an uncouth
gavel, insulting Jesus, apple pie and
family at every turn.

Now that was really something.

Once the embittered spy came in from the cold, he made
room for Bond, James Bond and his license to kill.
Kill a Commie for Mommy, sonny, and mother's milk was
Matt Helm,
        Mission: Impossible
        The Untouchables

Honey West
Hawaiian Eye
I Spy   The FBI
The Man from U.N.C.L.E.   The Girl from U.N.C.L.E.
T.H.E. Cat

Get Smart!
Our Man Flint
Lancelot Link: Secret Chimp.

Red Scare as real value.
Birth rate as replenishment.

And you can't keep a good flag down,

Burning or not.

Down to 30 Seconds of a Beat, Take 2
(For Steve Dalachinsky and the Unbearables)

It's life on the swing,

Up-beat, -down. Eyes glazed in the cluster lane,

Closing out the probing light;

> Heart stands down in surrender as hands take flight,

> Above, below, beyond said tempo, these years fall.

> Overtly on tacit, they writhe and wriggle.

> They sing…

Breathless, breathless,

No use to breathe,

Not time to see as

Curious clouds sound the shelter alarm.

Painting beyond, apart from the lines.

> It's not yet blue, dusk's mystery, twilight's hue

> And each flicker of black

> Leans deep into

> The pallet of sound

> A baptism, communion, head davening in prayer,

It's solemn, the song, enlightened by works.

Ancient, away, compulsion in stare,

The racing of shades, quilt not quite torn.

                    But spring never made it to here:

                     The infernal lickings at his heels,

               "There's people down here!", he cried.

"There's people down here", but none called back.

Can't be near, never be here.

        Never adhere.

            "There's people down here!"

            Forever be embers

               Blinding the seer,

            Ever the stand.

            Always we'll be.

            Always we'll be.

New Birth
(For the Abraham Lincoln Battalion, XVth Brigade)

Rúmbala, rúmbala, rúmbala!

The fight has

The fight has just begun

Just begun

Rúmbala, rúmbala, rúmbala!

Just begun

This final conflict, the march for reason,

The fight against fascism---

begun

Anew.

To you, to you, to you beloved comrades

who sang the people's song,

fought and fell in

the first

People's war

De los cuatro muleros

Mamita mía

Rumbala, rumbala

    Que van al campo,

        Al campo

Jarama is here.

Jarama is now. Jarama eternal.

The List. The 10. Phone-taps.

Smoke, mirrors, spying eyes;

Thought's a crime and

Labor reviled.

Where you stood, we stand now,

Jarama is here.

Coup de Franco, Fascist Right;

This fight is ours

Forces rise!

El de la mula torda

Mamita mía

Moreno y alto,

Moreno y alto

                              The fight, the fight goes on.

Rúmbala, rúmbala, rúmbala!

Revolution is strife between

What was and to be

Our present tense, our present, now.

Popular Front decreed.

                              Code Noir, minstrel show

                                 Sambo, old Jim Crow,

                       All come out for the lynching show!

                              The fight, still. The fight. Still.

                                 Rúmbala, rúmbala, rúmbala!

Manipulations of CIA,

Timeless today.

Humiliation,

Segregation,

Evisceration, deportation.

                       Dreamers awoken, Dreamers awake!

                       But it's the same dream, the same dream.

                                   Night raids, dark extreme,

                                           Night terrors and

                          Blue hours for the different, the new.

Side-eyed glancing blows,

Powdered frost over who's forgotten,

The frozen.

Those apart,

The OTHER. Ay, Manuela.

                                   The fight was then, the fight

                                          Renewed. The fight

                                                   Renewed.

                                    Ay, Manuela, ay, Manuela

                                  Rúmbala, rúmbala, rúmbala!

Brownshirts,

detention camps

Official, devised.

Royalty surmised.

White pride.

White national,

Supremacy.

White Hate.

        The Alpha. Decider. Breadwinner. Mr. Mister.

                The Man. Supreme.

          Domination. The little woman, bitch,

         ball-and-chain, the fairer sex, T and A.

       They'll let you do anything when you're a celebrity.

Now, here comes the Highway Patrol

Beating farmers from the Dustbowl.

Pinkerton thugs kill with

Fire and gun and stone.

When we were all hungry. When we were

All alone.

Blame the poor for lack of home.

         RESERVATIONS: Lock-up our Nations

             Native lands' desecration.

         Winter water cannons snarl and bite,

Claim the land and bleed

Tradition.

Camps for the Japanese citizen,

J. Edgar HUAC in secret drag

Deporting Reds,

    The scare is back;

        Ay…..

CO-INTEL, Liberte,

Hollywood 10, Chicago 8

Central Park 5, Free Bobby Seale,

Free Angela Davis from

Prison Industrial's Complex

The fight, the fight goes on.

Drug sweep, profile,

Muslim ban, No Irish Need Apply.

Joe Hill, Kevin Barry, Sacco,

Tom Mooney,

Scottsboro, Vanzetti.

The Wobs, the Party.

> Emma Goldman. And Paul Robeson.

> Trumbo. The Rosenbergs.

Herndon. Peltier. Mumia, Amiri. Panthers, Lords,

> Weathermen. Lennon, NOW, ACT-UP,

> Guerilla Girls, Teamsters and Turtles

> Stopping gears.

> Silencing the silencing.

Moneychangers stealing lives, breaking pride

Stacking courts, toppling elections.

Feeding on promise,

Hate crimes all the rage, and

> The cold

> grows colder by the day.

> Disrupt, divide,

> Repeal denied.

> And the fight must go on.

> The fight must still go on.

      Rúmbala, rúmbala, rúmbala!

New birth, new birth

When we have won, when we have won.

Acabar con el fascismo

Ay, Manuela,

Ay, Manuela

      Broken mirrors splintered

        Shards of

        Constitution,

      Un-American perseveration.

       Viva la quince brigade…

      Rúmbala, rúmbala, rúmbala!

When we have won-----

  Que se ha cubierta de gloria,

    Ay, Manuela,

     Ay, Manuela!

       New birth, new birth

       When we have won,

when we have won,

when we have won.

When we have won,

Rúmbala, rúmbala, rúmbala!

.........................Till we outnumber 'em.

JOHN PIETARO is a writer, poet, spoken word artist and musician from Brooklyn, NY. His publications include poetry collections *A Bleeding in Black Leather* (Uncollected Press, 2022), *The Mercer Stands Burning: Night Poems* (Atmosphere Press 2020), and the 2019 chapbook *Smoke Rings*. Earlier, Pietaro penned contemporary proletarian fiction set *Night People & Other Tales of Working New York* (2013) and contributed a chapter to Paul Buhle and Harvey Pekar's *SDS: A Graphic History* (Hill & Wang 2007). He also wrote multiple entries for the upcoming edition of *The Encyclopedia of the American Left* (Verso) and is currently deep into first novel *Of Seconds and Shadows*. Pietaro's creative writing has appeared in numerous international anthologies and journals.

Staff writer of *The NYC Jazz Record*, Pietaro is a contributing arts reporter to *PleaseKillMe*, *The Wire* (UK), *Z*, *Sensitive Skin*, *AllAboutJazz*, *The Nation*, *The Village Sun*, *Counter Punch*, *People's World*, *TruthOut* and others, and he was among the honorees at the New York Press Association 2021 "Better Newspaper" awards ceremony for his obit of drummer Deep Pop in *The Village Sun*.

Pietaro founded the Dissident Arts and Brecht Lives! festivals, co-hosts weekly radio show "Beneath the Underground" (WFMU.org), and fronts poetry/punk jazz ensemble the Red Microphone, recording artists of the ESP-Disk label. The band's latest, *A Bleeding in Black*

Leather, released 2022, featured guest trumpeter Mac Gollehon. Prior, the band released *And I Became of the Dark* with guests baritone saxophonist Claire Daley and violist Gwen Laster, and collaborated with poet/activist Amina Baraka for *Amina Baraka & the Red Microphone* (2017). Ms. Baraka also performed Pietaro's "Her Side of the Road" as a dramatic reading in 2018.

A guest speaker at Left Forum, the Vision Festival and People's Music Network convergence, Pietaro has been featured at the NYC Poetry Festival, Song of Myself Marathon, Boog City Festival, the International Human Rights Arts Festival, Great Weather for Media's Spoken Word Sundays, Workers United Film Festival, UpSurge JazzPoetry Festival and many others. He holds membership in the Authors Guild, the Poetry Society of New York, the National Writers Union, and International Federation of Journalists.

As a spoken word artist or percussionist, Pietaro has collaborated with Allen Ginsberg, Pete Seeger, Amina Baraka, Karl Berger, George Wallace, Steve Dalachinsky, Nora Guthrie, Ras Moshe, Erika Dagnino, William Hooker, the Flames of Discontent, historians Paul Buhle and Will Kaufman, and record producers Ivan Julian and Kramer, among many more. A life-long activist, he's been working within the labor movement since 2002, and prior was employed in social services during the AIDS crisis.

JohnPietaro.com   TheCulturalWorker.blogspot.com

MORE ROADSIDE PRESS TITLES:

By Plane, Train or Coincidence
Michele McDannold

Prying
Jack Micheline, Charles Bukowski and Catfish McDaris

Wolf Whistles Behind the Dumpster
Dan Provost

*Busking Blues: Recollections of a Chicago Street Musician
and Squatter*
Westley Heine

Unknowable Things
Kerry Trautman

How to Play House
Heather Dorn

Kiss the Heathens
Ryan Quinn Flanagan

St. James Infirmary
Steven Meloan

Street Corner Spirits
Westley Heine

A Room Above a Convenience Store
William Taylor Jr.

Resurrection Song
George Wallace

Nothing and Too Much to Talk About
Nancy Patrice Davenport

MORE ROADSIDE PRESS TITLES:

Bar Guide for the Seriously Deranged
Alan Catlin

Born on Good Friday
Nathan Graziano

Under Normal Conditions
Karl Koweski

The Dead and the Desperate
Dan Denton

Clown Gravy
Misti Rainwater-Lites

Walking Away
Michael D. Grover

All in a Pretty Little Row
Dan Provost

These Are the People in Your Neighbourhood
Jordan Trethewey

They Said I Wasn't College Material
Scot Young

Radio Water
Francine Witte

And Blackberries Grew Wild
Susan Mickelberry

Licorice Heart
Miles Budimir

Disposable Darlings
Todd Cirillo

Full Moon Midnight
Belinda Subraman